Politics and Propaganda

ADAM HIBBERT

W
FRANKLIN WATTS
LONDON•SYDNEY

First published in 2004 by Franklin Watts
96 Leonard Street, London EC2A 4XD

Franklin Watts Australia
45-51 Huntley Street
Alexandria, NSW 2015

Series editor: Rachel Cooke
Design: Storeybooks
Series design: White Design
Picture research: Diana Morris

Acknowledgements:
Austrian Archives/Corbis: 9t. BESIP: 19b. Bettmann/Corbis: 17bl, 23t.
David Cumming/Corbis: 18b. Wang Dingchang/Xinhua/Corbis: 27t.
EPA/PA: 14bl. Owen Franken/Corbis: 28. Mark Godfrey/Image Works/
Topham: 26. Tim Graham/Sygma/Corbis: 17tr. Farrell Grehan/Corbis: 5.
Hulton Deutsch/Corbis: 7, 19t. Ed Kashi/Corbis: 24. David King: 9bl, 9br.
Helen King/Corbis: 15. Patrick Kovarick/AFP/Getty: 20c. Brooks Kraft/Corbis: 20b.
Francoise de Mulder/Corbis: 11. PA/Topham: 10. David Pollack/Corbis: 25t.
Roger Ressmeyer/Corbis: 16. Rex Features: 4, 22, 23b, 27b, 29.
Ricki Rosen/Corbis: 6. Ron Sachs/Rex Features: front cover, 12.
Boustani Samara/Sygma/Corbis: 25b. Joesph Sohm/Visions of America/Corbis: 21.
Ted Spiegel/Corbis: 8. Orban Thierry/Sygma/Corbis: 13. UPPA/Topham: 14tr.

A CIP catalogue record for this book is available from the British Library.

ISBN: 0 7496 5784 7

Printed in Belgium

CONTENTS

⬆ *People can demonstrate their political ideas by taking to the streets – in a demonstration. These people are demonstrating in Genoa, Italy, against the actions of international businesses.*

POLITICS IS THE WORK OF deciding how to run a society. It usually includes a battle over different ideas about what that society should do. It always includes competition between the different people who want to be in charge. The political battle to win voters' support creates many of the stories we see in the media – in newspapers and on television.

DEMOCRACY

Democracy is an Ancient Greek word which means 'rule by the people'. It describes a society that involves everyone in politics, not just the powerful. People who want to be in charge in a democratic country have to win support from a large part of the population, instead of grabbing power by force.

PARTY

Democratic countries have governments which are made up of elected politicians. To organise a government, politicians have to work together as a team, known as a political party. Each party has a set of ideas which it offers to the voters, to win their support. The party that wins the most votes gains control of the government and puts its ideas into action.

VOTERS

Parties gain power in a democracy by winning an election. Voters decide which party they think is most likely to achieve their goals. They elect, or choose, the person or party that suits them. All the votes are added up, and the party with the most votes wins the election. Some systems give all the power to the winner. Others share some power with the runners-up.

⬇ *Small groups of people vote on decisions by raising their hands. These agricultural workers in the USA are voting whether to strike, or stop work, for more pay.*

MEDIA AND POLITICS

Most people rarely meet a politician in their daily lives. Instead, they read newspapers or watch television news to find out what politicians are doing and saying. This gives the media an important role in society. Voters rely on the media for the information to base their decisions on. If that information is biased or limited, it may prejudice votes.

GET THE FACTS STRAIGHT

Leading democracies have strong laws defending their media from political control – so-called freedom of speech. This protects democracies from being dominated by one person or group. But, according to research by Freedom House (see page 31), not all countries have the same level of free speech.

	rights in constitution	rights in court	journalists not bullied	internet freedom	many media owners
New Zealand	✓	✓	✓	✓	✓
Denmark	✓	✓	✓	✓	✓
Australia	✗	✓	–	–	–
Netherlands	✓	✓	–	✓	✗
UK	✗	–	✗	–	✓
USA	✓	✓	–	–	✓
France	✓	✓	–	✓	✓
Italy	✓	✗	✗	✓	✗

✓ = good   - = average   ✗ = poor

WHAT IS PROPAGANDA?

TO CALL SOMETHING 'PROPAGANDA'

is to say that it comes from a particular viewpoint, or serves a political goal. Political ideas have to be 'sold' to the public. Propaganda includes all the activities that people use to persuade others to support them. It is an important part of any working democracy but there are an amazing number of ways that a simple message can be passed to the public.

HONEST

Politicians can simply say what their beliefs are, and leave the public to make up their own minds about the message. This is the simplest type of propaganda – straight argument. It is what most people experience in daily life when they talk about political topics with each other.

A supporter and a critic of the Israeli government use straight arguments to try to persuade each other to change their political beliefs.

STYLISH

A good argument can be lost in politics because the person doing the arguing does not seem as confident or attractive as their opponent. So politicians practise how they speak, or change how they look, to add to their appeal. They may also try to be seen in stylish locations, such as celebrity events, fashion shows or exclusive holiday resorts. This helps to make them seem attractive.

TRICKY

Even good, stylish arguments can be lost if your opponent uses tricks to weaken your message – for example, spreading a rumour about you which stops the public treating you seriously. In 2002, the 58-year-old German leader Gerhard Schroeder had to take court action to end rumours that he dyed his hair – the rumour was making him a target for ridicule.

FAKE

Propaganda can sometimes include deceiving people, to trick them into agreeing with a certain idea. This type of propaganda is sometimes used in wartime, for example to convince enemy troops that they are closer to defeat than they actually are. It is used more often in societies without a free media, which might otherwise discover and expose the lie.

➡ *In Europe in the early 20th century, stories and pictures that pretended that Jewish people harmed Christian children were common. Their aim was to fuel hatred of the Jews.*

WHAT DO YOU THINK?

Some propaganda is obviously bad – for example, German Nazi Party cartoons which imagined Jewish people drinking the blood of German children (see below). The race hate message uses a certain style – nightmarish fantasy – to make its point. Is there anything about this style which should warn us to be suspicious of the message it contains? If this cartoon's style was used for a different message – for example, arms traders drinking the blood of African child soldiers – do you think it would be more acceptable? Why, or why not?

PROPAGANDA IS AS OLD *as politics itself. Once people began to group together by choice, rather than out of fear of violence, it became important for leaders to be able to persuade others to follow them. Modern propaganda is quite different, though: it is based on scientific methods which were not discovered until the 20th century.*

BIRTH OF DEMOCRACY

The first attempt at a democratic society happened in the Ancient Greek city state of Athens, around 2,500 years ago. All the full citizens of the city (property-owning males born locally) were involved in the political decisions of the city. The Greeks soon noticed that there was a special skill to persuading and arguing with people, which they called the art of rhetoric.

Ancient Greek thinkers such as Plato (pointing up) and Aristotle (gesturing down) discovered the rules of rhetoric – and getting a message across.

LATIN WORD

The word 'propaganda' comes from Latin, and means helping something to grow and spread. We use the Latin word because the Roman Catholic church was one of the first organisations to have a special section for spreading its beliefs, called the *Congregatio de Propaganda Fide* – the Congregation for the Propagation of the Faith – which was created around 380 years ago.

MASS MEDIA

Modern propaganda dates from around the same time as the Catholic Congregatio. It was then that the invention of the printing press made newspapers possible. Competition for power in Europe, especially between Catholics and Protestants, led to the printing of thousands of newspapers and newsletters arguing for one side or another. Printed news is still extremely important for propaganda.

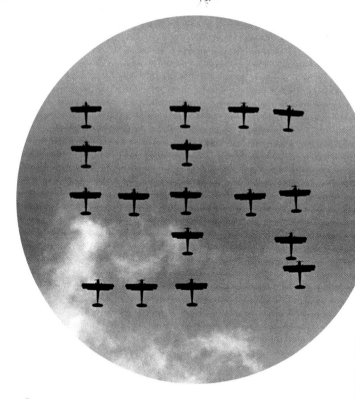

WIRELESS WORDS

Every new media technology creates a new 'stage' which politicians can use to reach their audience. For example, radio technology was invented around 1900, and perfected in the 1920s. In the 1930s, Adolf Hitler's Ministry of Public Enlightenment and Propaganda in Germany used the radio to persuade Germans to support his rule.

FACING THE ISSUES

As people get used to a new form of media, they have to learn to recognise the tricks that can be used by a propagandist. In the Soviet Union in the early 20th century, for example, photographs were still so new and 'scientific' that people believed exactly what they showed. But the Soviet government changed photographs to exclude people, such as Leon Trotsky, that they did not approve of. Soviet citizens began to doubt the truth of photographs and the messages that they conveyed.

⬆ *The Nazi party used aircraft to create this flying swastika symbol – identifying the party with new technology.*

⬇ *When Leon Trotsky fell out with the Soviet government, it doctored this and other official photographs to remove him. He is the lower of the two figures ringed in the left-hand picture missing in the doctored right-hand one.*

THE SIMPLEST STYLE of propaganda is the 'personality cult'. The dictator or ruler puts out pictures of himself, and the image of his face appears everywhere – in schools, on the sides of buildings and in thousands of posters. This sort of propaganda can sometimes convince children and young people to trust the leader and to follow his orders.

ANCIENT TRICK

One of the oldest pieces of propaganda we have is an Egyptian record of a battle between Egypt and the Hittite people over 3,000 years ago. The ruler of Egypt, Ramses II, is described as defeating the entire Hittite army on his own! This news was meant to make him seem more like a god than a person to the people he ruled, and to Egypt's enemies.

TOPPLING THE ICON

Saddam Hussein, the dictator of Iraq from 1979-2003, was thrown out of power by an American-led military invasion. The occupation of the Iraqi capital, Baghdad, was marked by a famous TV event, in which a statue of the dictator was pulled down. The destruction of this symbol of the old regime showed everyone that the regime was gone. It turned Hussein's symbolic power against him.

← Some Iraqis celebrated the defeat of the Ba'ath regime by American-led forces by vandalising images of Saddam Hussein on their public buildings.

ONE FACE RULES

The personality cult is useful for another important reason. It does not really matter to a dictator whether the people love or hate him. If the leader is the only part of the government the people recognise, removing him risks destroying law and order completely, as happened in Iraq in 2003. This forces other powerful people in the country, especially military commanders, to be extremely wary of challenging the leader.

SYMBOLS

In Cuba, a personality cult has grown up around Che Guevara, one of the leaders of the 1958 rebellion which created Cuba's socialist government. Guevara was killed in 1967 while helping rebels in Bolivia. His image became a simple way for the Cuban government to inspire its citizens to work selflessly for 'the revolution', for which people like Guevara gave their lives.

➡ *Che Guevara is shown as a brave rebel soldier to inspire Cubans at a ceremony marking the birth of the Socialist Republic of Cuba.*

WHAT DO YOU THINK?

Personality cults may seem foolish from the viewpoint of a democratic country, but are we free of them? Modern political leaders have to present themselves and their families very carefully. Many voters make political judgements according to whether they feel a politician has a likeable personality or not. Does this amount to a sort of personality cult, or perhaps personality propaganda?

↑ *These American citizens are attending a political rally. Speeches at the rally give them new ideas for persuading their friends and workmates to vote for their party.*

IN DEMOCRATIC COUNTRIES, *voters decide what to believe by listening to the opinions of their friends, workmates, family, politicians, websites, experts, newspapers, radio and TV programmes. Propaganda which aims to change how voters think has to be well designed, to influence as many of these levels of opinion as possible.*

24-HOUR NEWS

TV and internet news stories change around the clock. Politicians compete to turn stories towards their own point of view. This competition forces them to keep an eye on the news, work out responses to stories, and contact news media quickly to get their opinions in first. This work is called media relations, or 'media management'.

THE PROFESSIONALS

Politicians and political parties employ experts to help them get the most out of the media. These are called press officers or public relations (PR) officers. Press officers are often people who have been journalists – they understand what the media needs to make a good news story. Most have friends working in the media, giving them a better chance of getting their stories noticed.

WELL-GROOMED

Political leaders are expected to look happy, healthy and calm at all times. Experts called image consultants help to keep up this appearance. Image consultants may choose a politician's clothes, make sure their 'look' is appealing to voters, train them how to move around, and make sure they have just enough make-up on to look good under the bright lights of TV cameras.

GET THE FACTS STRAIGHT

If one media company owns too many TV channels, newspapers and websites, voters may only hear one side of a story. So democracies try to limit media companies from having too much influence within one country. This forces growing media companies to look for their next customers in other countries around the globe, creating global media 'empires'. Some people are concerned that this globalisation has its own limiting effects on press freedom as they are run by people with their own political agenda.

Top Media Empires:	US$ billion sales, 2003
Time Warner	41
Walt Disney	25
Viacom	25
News Corporation	19
NBC Universal	14 (estimated)
Bertelsmann	9
Sony (media divisions)	9

A make-up artist prepares the French right-wing leader, Jean Marie Le-Pen, for a TV appearance.

DIFFERENT GROUPS OF VOTERS

pay attention to different sorts of propaganda. So politicians try to choose a style to suit each audience. For example, if they are writing a piece for a serious newspaper, their readers will want to see strong political arguments. For a radio or TV news programme, they need to say something simple that everyone can remember and repeat easily.

↗ As Prime Minister of the UK, Tony Blair used skills such as guitar-playing and playing football to show that he was an ordinary, likeable person.

← Spanish socialist leader José Zapatero visited emergency workers at an oil spill in 2002, using this news story to reach a new audience.

GETTING ATTENTION

Propaganda does not work if its message is about something that does not matter to voters. So an important part of designing propaganda is deciding which issues matter and focusing any campaign on these. For instance, messages about the money we earn and the level of crime we face seem more important to most adults than other issues, such as how our society might pay for public libraries.

HOW INTERESTED?

Politicians have to be able to judge how interested their audience is in a political message. If they are only slightly interested, a brief, punchy comment will do better than a long, complicated one. On a chat show such as Oprah or Parkinson, the best propaganda may be to say nothing political – just trying to be nice and friendly may win the politician more supporters than political debate could.

FOCUS GROUPS

When people feel strongly about an issue, it may be hard to make them consider a new idea related to it. Some politicians use focus groups. A handful of people from all walks of life are gathered in a room and asked to respond to some different messages. Politicians can study their responses to see which way of presenting the message works best.

FACING THE ISSUES

Propaganda makers have to stay in touch with what their audience – known as 'reactors' – are interested in. In the USA, for example, citizens became less interested in foreign news throughout the 1980s and 1990s. From 1983 to 1998, foreign news coverage in major US newspapers fell from 10% to 2% of the available space, while TV news coverage of foreign stories fell from 45% of news stories in 1975 to 13.5% in 1995. For politicians during this period, foreign issues became a less useful way to appeal to voters.

⬇ *In this focus group, a researcher is testing how a section of the population (male, working age) will react to a range of political ideas .*

CHOOSING WORDS

⬆ *Presenters on a TV news programme need politicians to talk in soundbites – giving them clips or phrases which fit neatly into a short news story.*

A POLITICAL MESSAGE *can be expressed in images, actions or words. Words are the most precise way to get a message across. As Ancient Greeks realised when they invented the art of rhetoric (see page 8), different styles of saying something can have a very different impact. One cleverly designed sentence may impress voters far more than a whole essay.*

DIFFERENT SPIN

The first step is to choose words which focus on the good (or bad) side of the subject being discussed. For example, compare these two ways to describe the same event:
• she used a private clinic to free herself of this unwanted pregnancy;
• she paid some hired assassins secretly to murder her unborn child.
These two different 'spins' on one event give very different ideas about its moral value, even though they describe the same event.

SOUNDBITE

TV and radio news programmes need a small 'clip' of a politician speaking, to show their audience what the politician was saying in a speech. Politicians deliberately create short phrases which sum up their message, called 'soundbites', for news media to repeat. Soundbites can be said again and again, by many politicians in one party. The repetition makes them easier for journalists to notice and report.

Australian political leader Paul Keating became well-known for his skill at labelling his political opponents, to make their ideas seem ridiculous.

LABELLING OPPONENTS

Sometimes politicians may need to demonstrate to their own team or to voters that they are tough, not afraid of a 'fight' with their opponents. For these sorts of reasons, politicians sometimes find it useful to bully or insult each other. For example, Australian politician Paul Keating said of one of his political enemies: 'He's like a shiver waiting for a spine.'

American civil rights leader Martin Luther King wrote his own speeches. It was partly his gift for words that made him an inspiring leader.

THE SPEECHWRITER

Designing messages in words can be a job for an expert, called a speechwriter. The speechwriter knows the art of rhetoric, understands the beliefs of the politician he or she works for, and suggests opportunities for the politician to use. Most presidents or prime ministers have speechwriters, or teams of speechwriters.

GET THE FACTS STRAIGHT

Almost any political idea can be presented as a statistic – a number which tells us something interesting about our world. For example, a government can say that crime statistics have fallen 5%, to 'prove' that its crime policy is succeeding. This statistic needs to be placed in context to be fully understood. If crime had already risen 20% since the government was elected, a 5% fall this year would not be as successful as it sounds. If victims of crime decided the police were corrupt and stopped reporting crimes, the 5% fall might be due to fewer reports, not better policing.

POLITICAL PARTIES *often use a logo, a small drawing, which is meant to express some of their beliefs. Images which stand for beliefs are called symbols. They appeal to us without using words. For this reason, symbols can play a powerful part in propaganda – they leave the precise meaning up to the person who sees the symbol.*

WHAT'S IN A SYMBOL?

Some symbols are more popular than others. One of the most widely-used symbols is the rainbow. Rainbows happen in nature as sunlight passes through rain, so they can be understood as meaning a promise for happier times ahead. The many colours within the rainbow form one curve, which can suggest respect for different lifestyles or ethnic groups.

FACING THE ISSUES

The German Nazi Party was one of the world's most efficient propaganda machines. It adopted a swastika from Hindu myth, to symbolise the ancient 'racial' roots of the German people. It forced Jews to wear a six-pointed star, so that they stuck out and were easier to bully. The swastika is now a banned symbol in Germany. In 2000, some 65-year-old trees were chopped down near Berlin when aerial photos showed that they had been planted to make a giant swastika on the landscape.

Greenpeace uses rainbow and dove symbols from the story of Noah's Ark, in the Bible, to express its ideals.

SIRIUS

CHILDREN

All human beings share powerful instincts to protect and care for children. So children make good symbols for many types of message. Politicians wanting to show voters that they are nice people like to be seen being kind to children. Showing that a person was not nice to a child can be a powerful way to make people distrust or hate the person.

HORROR STORIES

Terrible crimes can be used as symbols for political messages. The genocide (or 'holocaust') of European Jews in the 1940s is a symbol of evil which everyone recognises. In 2003, People for the Ethical Treatment of Animals (PeTA) was criticised for propaganda which tried to use this genocide as a symbol for the 'evil' of eating meat – PeTA's adverts were called 'The Holocaust On Your Plate'.

HEALTH CAMPAIGNS

Governments often issue propaganda to persuade people to take more care of their health. The health campaign against AIDS in the UK in the 1980s used a symbol of a gravestone to stand for the deadly disease. Together with the campaign slogan 'Don't die of ignorance', this propaganda had a dramatic effect on young people's attitudes to sex.

The German dictator Adolf Hitler liked to present himself as a friend to children. Seeing a male political leader like this can help to make citizens accept him as a 'father' figure.

This powerful image from the Czech government symbolises the damage drink-driving can do – a corkscrew used for unbottling wine is linked to a badly-crashed car.

PROPAGANDA ACTS

PEOPLE ARE USUALLY MORE

impressed by actions than by words. Everything that a government does has a propaganda effect, because it is reported in the media and interpreted, to see what it 'says' about political leaders. Sometimes it can seem as though a government has done something for the propaganda effect, not to achieve a real goal.

STUNTS AND DEMOS

Governments are not the only political actors who use actions to put a message across. Anyone can carry out an activity to send a political message. In December 2003, four Afghan refugees, detained on a Pacific island while seeking asylum in Australia, sewed their mouths shut and went on hunger strike. Their actions drew global media attention to the way they were being treated by the Australian authorities.

French president Chirac (left) and German chancellor Schroeder (right) share a drink after one European Union meeting – an act designed to show the two countries' friendship.

HANGING TOUGH

Governments can use their control of the armed forces to make powerful messages. During the invasion of Iraq in 2003, US President George W Bush wanted to stand together with the servicemen and women who were risking their lives on that mission. He asked journalists to film him in pilot's uniform, landing a military jet on a massive US warship, to show how involved he felt in the military effort.

US President George Bush did not fly a combat mission during the Iraq invasion in 2003. Flying a military jet was a propaganda act, to boost morale.

SPACE RACE

Competition between rival nations often involves 'propaganda acts'. The USSR scored a propaganda 'victory' against the USA in 1957 by being the first to launch a spacecraft into orbit, *Sputnik*. The USA had to do better, to show other countries that it was not falling behind the USSR. It poured money into space research, eventually winning the race to be first to put people on the Moon.

⬇ *The success of US astronauts is celebrated in a 'ticker tape' parade in New York. Their arrival on the Moon in 1969 was a powerful symbol of America's superiority over the USSR.*

GET THE FACTS STRAIGHT

A 'photo opportunity' is an event held by a politician or any other public figure, where photographers and TV camera crews are promised an interesting story. The politician invites the media to the event, and promises to be doing something that is worth reporting. The media has to decide which invitations to accept – if there are no big news stories already being worked on, they can rely on the photo opportunity to provide stories and images to fill any gaps.

There are fewer political stories during holidays. This 'silly season' makes it easier to get a story noticed.

WHEN JOURNALISTS WORKING ON news programmes and newspapers are deciding which stories to report, they look at what other journalists are reporting. This creates a shared 'news agenda', a set of headline stories that most newspapers and broadcasters will focus on each day. Politicians try to influence this agenda by placing stories in the right place at the right time.

WHAT DO YOU THINK?

Propaganda techniques such as the news management tricks on this page can seem dishonest. But politics is a contest or battle between different political groups and beliefs, with very few rules. Do you think you could 'win the battle' without using these tricks? Are some of them more honest or less honest than others? Who should set the rules for what counts as a 'fair fight' – the voters, or a judge?

The 'news agenda' of a day means that many papers will make the same story their headline news – such as all these French papers saluting the launch of the first French satellite.

TIMING NEWS

Politicians in government have an advantage – the media turns to them first for news. Governments can use this position to influence the 'news agenda'. For example, a politician times a big announcement so that the evening television news has time to make it a lead story. This evening TV news affects the headlines that newspapers choose to print overnight – setting the agenda for the following day.

CO-ORDINATION

Politicians have to check with each other to make sure that a success story they plan to talk about gets the best possible coverage from the media. They try to avoid releasing stories which will distract attention from the best news. Stories are timed so that each one gets its share of attention.

BURYING NEWS

Sometimes politicians have to admit to failure. But they can wait until the media are busy covering another big story – then their failure will not get much attention and will be 'buried'. On 11th September 2001, UK government adviser Jo Moore sent an email to civil servants which said: 'It's now a very good day to get out anything we want to bury.' The email was sent within hours of the massive terrorist attack on the USA.

OFF THE RECORD

Politicians can select journalists they trust, to reveal a story 'off the record'. This means that the journalist agrees to keep the politician's identity a secret, in return for an interesting story. Speaking 'off the record' makes it easier for politicians to use the media as a propaganda tool. Journalists state that such stories are from 'a source' to alert readers to this risk.

Jo Moore became notorious when her email was published. She later resigned.

23

IN TIMES OF WAR

An American soldier hands out leaflets in Arabic to Iraqi citizens in 2003, to persuade them to see US troops as friends – peace is symbolised with a dove.

EVEN IN VERY FREE, DEMOCRATIC
countries, propaganda becomes less honest in wartime – according to an old saying: 'Truth is the first casualty of war.' There are good and bad reasons for wartime propaganda. Just as opposing players in sports contests need to keep their plans secret, opposing countries in a war try very hard to hide information from the enemy.

NATIONAL SECURITY

Governments may need to lie in wartime in order to keep plans secret. For example, in the First World War, thousands of British transport workers thought they were delivering water tanks to the battlefront in Belgium. The truth about these 'tanks', which were really the first armoured fighting vehicles, was only revealed when they launched a surprise attack on German lines in 1916.

FACING THE ISSUES

Armed forces learn from each other's experience about how to manage news. For example, Lt Commander Arthur Humphries of the US Navy wrote this report on British news management in the Falklands War of 1982: 'In the Falklands the British failed to appreciate that news management is more than just ... censorship. It also means providing pictures.' In the 2003 Iraq war, journalists were allowed to report from within US-led military units. Under military supervision, they reported the soldiers' view of the invasion of Iraq - with plenty of pictures.

Posters from the Second World War remind people of the dangers of information reaching the enemy.

HOME FRONT

Wars in the modern world rely on people at home as well as soldiers in the field. Political leaders try to make sure the public hear about military successes, and also try to keep stories about military defeats or accidents out of the headlines. This encourages people to support the war and contribute to it – for example, by sending friendly messages of support to the troops.

PSYCHOLOGICAL OPERATIONS

Propaganda can be aimed at enemy soldiers, to trick them or to tell them facts their own commanders would prefer to keep secret. This is known as 'psychological operations', or PsyOps. Like other propaganda, PsyOps often include actions as well as words. A huge missile attack on Iraq in 2003 was called 'Shock and Awe'. It was designed to show Iraqi soldiers that they had no hope of winning.

Kuwaiti propaganda in 1990 claimed that Iraqi troops stole incubators, such as this one, leaving Kuwaiti babies to die.

WINNING ALLIES

In 1990, Kuwaiti leaders needed to persuade the USA to free their country from an Iraqi invasion. They created a fake story about babies being murdered by Iraqi soldiers. The Kuwaiti ambassador's daughter posed as an eye witness to the atrocity. As we saw on page 19, children and babies make powerful symbols. Outrage at this story helped to persuade the American people to support the war.

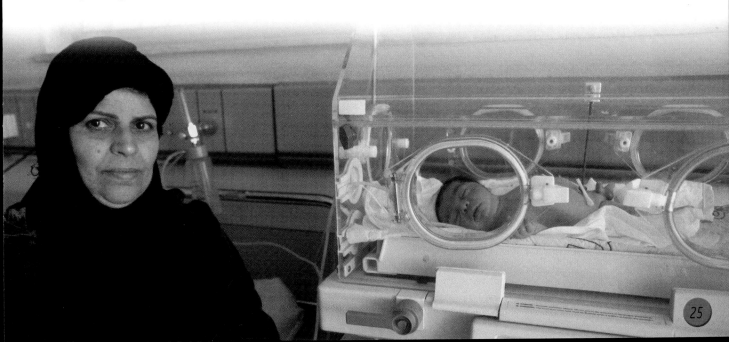

PROPAGANDA CAN BE HARMFUL to

society. If large numbers of people are fooled by a false piece of propaganda, this can be very bad for democracy. So democracies try to set rules which act as limits to the power of propaganda. They are all aimed at making sure that the public hears more than one side to any story – especially so that the government is not able to control the news.

FREE PRESS

If the government controls what the media can say, it can control the political messages people hear. But most societies want some controls – for example, to stop companies lying about their products in advertisements. Each democracy finds its own balance on this question (see the table on page 5). All agree that journalists should not be threatened by police or government officials.

FREE SPEECH

Beyond the media, democracies try to guarantee people the right to believe what they want, and to express those beliefs. In democracies it is legal to express almost any belief, though the rules vary from country to country. In the last 30 years, beliefs concerning drug use and sex have become less controlled, while beliefs which express 'hatred' for minorities tend to be more controlled.

WHAT DO YOU THINK?

Do you or your family prefer a particular news channel or newspaper? Does it cover the news neutrally, or does it tend to approve of opinions from one side of political debates? If you were to buy a newspaper, would you buy one written by people whose political beliefs you share? Would you be happy to read a paper regularly which expressed political beliefs that offend or irritate you? After thinking about these questions, do you think you see all sides of a debate?

⬅ *These journalists are watching a US President resign as a result of a scandal they revealed to the public.*

The argument between the UK government and the BBC led some people who were against the war in Iraq to accuse the prime minister, Tony Blair, of being a liar – in this case, playing with his name to make their point.

FACING THE ISSUES

In 2003, the UK government and the British Broadcasting Company (BBC) argued over the accuracy of a BBC story which involved secret intelligence on Iraqi weapons – a key piece of information in the UK's decision to go to war against Iraq. Control of information is used by all governments as a security measure. In democracies, the public expects to know everything the government knows, unless there is a very strong security reason – such as keeping spies' identities a secret – to hold information back. But only governments can decide which secrets to reveal and which to keep. This made it hard for the British public to decide whether the government or the BBC was in the right.

BELIEF BIAS

There is disagreement over what counts as propaganda, so we try to avoid presenting beliefs as 'the truth' in schools or other state-run spaces, such as law courts. Beliefs are meant to be left to open discussion, and public spaces are meant to make no assumptions about which beliefs a citizen might have. This sometimes leads to controversy over, for example, religion in schools.

Muslims worship outside in Nice, France. The gathering was part of a protest over the French government's decision to ban Muslim girls from wearing head scarves at school.

GET THE FACTS STRAIGHT

The number of possible voters who actually cast their vote in an election remained stable throughout the Cold War period, but took a sudden dip in the 1990s - indicating public disinterest in politics. This trend is visible across the world, although Denmark and Sweden appear to be unaffected.

Country	1950s	1960s	1970s	1980s	1990s	2000s
Austria	95.3	93.8	92.3	91.5	83.8	80.5
Canada	74.5	78.0	74.6	73.3	68.3	61.2
Denmark	81.7	87.3	88.4	86.7	84.4	87.2
Finland	76.5	85.0	78.2	73.9	67.4	69.6
France	80.0	76.6	76.5	71.8	68.0	64.4
Germany	86.9	87.1	90.9	87.3	79.6	79.1
Italy	93.8	92.8	92.3	88.9	85.5	81.4
Japan	73.7	69.8	71.9	71.3	61.5	59.0
Netherlands	95.4	95	83.5	83.5	76.0	79.5
New Zealand	94.7	89.1	86.0	91.4	85.5	76.9
Norway	78.8	82.8	81.6	83.1	76.9	75.0
Sweden	78.7	86.4	90.4	89.1	85.4	80.1
Switzerland	69.0	64.1	52.3	48.2	43.8	n/a
UK	80.2	76.6	75.0	74.1	74.6	59.4
USA(Presidential)	n/a	92.7	78.7	74.5	70.8	51.2
Aggregate trend:	77.3	83.8	80.8	79.2	74.1	67.0

Credit: Data from www.idea.int, 2003

Note: Australia is not included in this list as it is illegal there not to vote if you qualify to do so.

THE LARGEST TREND AFFECTING propaganda in the early 21st century is the decline in 'big ideas', and of public interest in politics. Political groups, parties, campaigns and other voluntary organisations are losing active members, throughout the developed world. This trend leaves politicians more and more separated from citizens - meaning that they will need the media's help to win our attention.

⊕ *Young people are less likely to be interested in political parties or voting.*

MEDIA SKILL

The huge range of media which voters meet in their daily lives – TV, radio, newspapers, magazines, internet, advertising, films, and so on – makes it hard for one voice to be noticed. Propaganda will become more 'scientific', to make it better at reaching a target audience. Political groups which have no propaganda experts will be unlikely to win widespread public support.

FEELINGS

As voters become less involved in politics, they will become more interested in private life. Politicians are beginning to recognise that trend in two different ways. Firstly, they allow the media to see more of their private lives, to present themselves as celebrities. Secondly, they will show their private emotions more in public – for example, shedding a tear in front of the cameras.

THE REAL THING?

As politicians become more like celebrities, talking less about their beliefs, some people will find them too 'fake' or 'unreal'. This could have two different effects. It might make voters even less likely to get involved with politics. It might also encourage voters to give more attention to anyone who is not a politician but who has powerful political opinions or emotions.

FAME FACTOR

The media decides what to report according to how interested people are in the story. If a story involves a famous celebrity, for example, the media knows that consumers or viewers will pay more attention. Some argue that this 'celebrity culture' leads to personality politics or even cults (page 10-11). It may make it easier for a politician with a strong personal style to take control of a democracy.

Arnold Schwarzenegger used his film-star status to attract voters. He was elected governor of California in 2003.

GLOSSARY

city state: Type of society from the ancient world, halfway between a tribe and a nation, based around a city.

civil rights: Rights of citizens to equality, especially in political freedoms such as free speech and voting.

democracy: Society in which government decisions are made by citizens, directly by voting, or indirectly by elected representatives.

demonstration: Political event demonstrating how many people support an idea, by gathering in public.

dictator: Leader who takes total control of a country's political system.

election: Round of voting to choose which person or political party should be in charge.

free speech: The right to talk or write about your beliefs, whatever they might be.

government: People who run a nation, that is political leaders and the officials they command.

journalist: Person researching, writing or presenting stories for print, TV, radio and web media.

media: Newspapers, TV and radio stations and other systems of mass communication.

morale: Spirit or mood, usually applied to armies – high morale gives the confidence to win.

Nazi: Political party in Germany in the 1930s and 1940s led by the dictator, Adolf Hitler.

news agenda: Story or stories which are headlines in most news media and create public interest.

party: Group of people of similar or identical political beliefs, organised to win political power.

politics: Activity to do with deciding who should run society, and how.

propaganda: Stories and arguments produced by a political group to persuade people to support it.

psychological operations: Military actions designed mainly to harm enemy morale.

rally: Event bringing political friends (allies) together to boost morale.

socialism: Political belief that suggests money and business should be controlled by a whole community, not just a wealthy elite.

society: A country, community or group of people, organised according to certain rules.

Soviet Union: Communist empire centred on Russia, including 14 neighbouring states (existed 1917-91).

spin: Twisting a news story to make it score political 'points' – like adding spin to a ball in sports such as tennis.

statistic: Fact involving numbers, which is calculated from a large body of evidence.

swastika: Symbol from Hindu mythology used by Nazi party to stand for Germany's ancient 'racial' roots.

symbol: Object, sign or action, which is used to communicate a meaning, or a value.

voter: Person with a right and responsibility to choose between political ideas and leaders in an election.

wireless: Radio set receiving broadcasts sent through the air, not down a wire.

CAMPAIGNING ORGANISATIONS

Freedom House
www.freedomhouse.org
US-based international organisation promoting freedom and democracy, and providing comparative data on countries across the globe.

Propaganda Critic
www.propagandacritic.com
An amateur-run site containing useful links to propaganda films, with thought-provoking articles about propaganda, and a useful index of propaganda techniques.

Article 19
www.article19.org
International campaign group defending free speech, named after the 'free speech' paragraph, or article, in the UN Universal Declaration of Human Rights. Publishes the Index on Censorship: www.indexonline.org

IFEX
www.ifex.org
The International Freedom of Expression Xchange connects campaigners for free speech in several languages and alerts online activists to new campaigns.

Fair
www.fair.org
US-based Fairness and Accuracy In Reporting discusses media coverage and 'spin' on leading stories. The website's Counterspin section and 9.11 Archive are useful.

INTERNATIONAL ORGANISATIONS

International Federation of Journalists
www.ifj.org
A global federation of journalists and journalists' unions which aims to ensure that the media is free everywhere in the world to speak the truth.

MAGIC
www.unicef.org/magic
Media Activities and Good Ideas by, with and for Children is UNICEF's resource for young people to investigate their rights and talk to like-minded people around the world.

IDEA
www.idea.int
International Institute for Democracy and Electoral Assistance is a club of countries around the world who help each other maintain the best democratic standards.

MEDIA AND ARCHIVES

National Archive (USA)
www.archives.gov
A huge archive of American government publications, including wartime propaganda posters.

PsyWar Society
www.psywarsoc.org
A fascinating archive of propaganda leaflets dropped during various wars as part of psychological operations, to undermine enemy morale.

Pew Research Centre
people-press.org
Great resource for investigating the relationship between voter behaviour, propaganda and the media.

INDEX